Barnstaple

Webster's Timeline History 1154 - 2006

Webster's Online Dictionary

(www.websters-online-dictionary.org)

Published by ICON Group International, Inc.
7404 Trade Street
San Diego, California 92121

www.icongrouponline.com

This edition published by ICON Group International, Inc. in 2009
Printed in the United States of America.

Barnstaple: Webster's Timeline History, 1154 - 2006

ISBN 0-546-86690-5

PREFACE

Webster's bibliographic and event-based timelines are comprehensive in scope, covering virtually all topics, geographic locations and people. They do so from a linguistic point of view, and in the case of this book, the focus is on "Barnstaple," including when used in literature (e.g. all books that might have "Barnstaple" in their title). As such, this book represents the largest compilation of timeline events associated with "Barnstaple". Webster's timelines cover bibliographic citations, patented inventions, as well as non-conventional and alternative meanings which capture ambiguities in usage. These furthermore cover all parts of speech (possessive, institutional usage, geographic usage) and contexts, including pop culture, the arts, social sciences (linguistics, history, geography, economics, sociology, political science), business, computer science, literature, law, medicine, psychology, mathematics, chemistry, physics, biology and other physical sciences. The following keywords were used to build the timeline: Barnstaple. This "data dump" results in a comprehensive set of entries for a bibliographic and/or event-based timeline on the word "Barnstaple", since editorial decisions to include or exclude events is purely a linguistic process. The resulting entries are used under license or with permission, used under "fair use" conditions, used in agreement with the original authors, or are in the public domain. Across all of the Webster's timelines, at the end of some entries the following codes are used to identify certain sources: [WP] Wikipedia.org. All entries marked [WP] are adapted from articles created by contributors to Wikipedia.org, the free encyclopedia under a copyleft GNU Free Documentation License (GFDL) based on the headword. Please note that these entries are not full articles. For the full article associated with a given Wikipedia headword, the reader can simply go to www.wikipedia.org or www.websters-online-dictionary.org and type in the name of the topic to better understand the context of the entry; passages attributed to Wikipedia are exempt from any compilation or other copyright held by this book and can be freely used under the GFDL found at www.wikipedia.org. The full GFDL is reproduced at the end of the book before the index, and applies to each Wikipedia headword in any of the Webster's Timelines. For all of the sources, the original authors holding copyright retain any copyrights. Proceeds from this book are used to expand the content and coverage of Webster's Online Dictionary (www.websters-online-dictionary.org).

1154

Lundy: Exactly when the Templars were first given the island is uncertain but it would seem that as they were a major maritime force in the reign of King Henry II (1154-1189), he gave them Lundy as an English port of refuge. Whether they actually took possession of the island then is questionable, though the Order did have economic interests in north Devon and may well have been given the island as an alternative to the Taw river landings leading to Barnstaple. It has been speculated that one of the reasons for the king's generosity was that the Norsemen were troubling Scotland and may have posed a threat to more southern waters. [WP]

1596

Peter Wentworth: Peter Wentworth (1530 - November 10, 1596) was the elder brother of Paul Wentworth, and like his brother was a prominent puritan leader in parliament, which he first entered as member for Barnstaple in 1571. [WP]

1609

DU MOULIN. the Elder. Pierre: Publication of "Heraclitus: or meditations upon the vanity and misery of humane life, first written in French by. P. D. M. and translated into English by R. S., Gentleman (i.e. Richard Smyth, of Barnstaple)." Published in 1609.

1610

Smyth, Richard, preacher in Barnstaple, Devonshire: Publication of "Munition against mans misery & mortality: A treatice containing the most effectuall remedies against the miserable state of man in this life, selected out of the chiefest both humane and divine authors; by Richard Smyth preacher of Gods word in Barstaple in Devonshire." Publisher: printed by Ioseph Barnes (At Oxford). Published in 1610.

1612

Smyth, Preacher in Barnstaple, Devonshire. Richard: Publication of "Munition against mans miserie and mortality. Second edition." Published in 1612.

1616

Carpenter, Richard: Born in 1575 and died in 1627, authored "A pastoral charge : Faithfully giuen and discharged, at the trienniall visitation of the Lord Bishop of Exon: holden in Barnstaple the seuenth of September, 1616. By Richard Carpenter pastor of Sherwill in Devon. (Christs larumbell of loue resounded.) (Christs larumbell of love resounded.)." Publisher: printed by Edvvard Griffin for Francis Constable dvvelling at the white Lyon in Pauls Churchyard (London). Published in 1616.

John Loosemore: John Loosemore was born in Barnstaple where he was baptized on August 25, 1616. His father was also a builder and repairer of organs, and passed on the trade to his son John, who moved to Exeter sometime before 1645. The other two sons of the family, Henry and George, also had a connection with organ music as they were eventually appointed organists at King's College, Cambridge and Trinity College, Cambridge, respectively, probably under the patronage of Dudley North, 4th Baron North. [WP]

1617

Church of England. Archdeaconry of Barnstaple: Publication of "Articles to bee enquired of by the church-wardens and sworne-men within the arch-deaconrie of Barnestaple, in the diocesse of Exeter,: in the visitation there holden in the yeare of our lord God. 1617." Publisher: printed by Thomas Purfoot., An. Dom (At London). Published in 1617.

1634

Smyth, Richard, preacher in Barnstaple,

1646

Devonshire: Publication of "Munition against mans miserie and mortalitie : a treatise containing the most effectuall remedies against the miserable state of man in this life, selected out of the chiefest both humane and divine authors." By Richard Smith preacher of Gods Word in Barstaple (sic) in Devonshire. Publisher: printed for William Turner (Oxford). Published in 1634.

1646

Publication: Publication of "Foure strong castles taken by the Parliaments forces:: with the copies of the severall articles, and letters of the particulars thereof. 1 Titbury Castle (in Staffordshire) taken by Sir William Brereton, with all the armes and ammunition. 2 Dunster Castle (in the west) taken by Col. Blake, with all the armes, ammunition, and other furniture of warre. 3 The copie of the articles for the surrender of Barnstaple, with all the ordnance, ammunition, bag and baggage. 4. Abarstwith Castle (in Wales) taken by Col. Powell, with all their armes, ammunition, bag and baggage. Also the agreement for the sleighting of Barton Garrison in Derbishire neere Titbury, and Sir VVilliam Breretons proceedings against Lichfield Close, with the copie of a letter from Sir VVilliam Breretons quarters. Being the true copies of the originals, published according to order of Parliament." Publisher: printed for Matthew Walbancke at Grayes Inne Gate., Aprill 27 (London). Published in 1646.

Torshell, Samuel: Author of "The Palace of Justice opened and set to view; in a sermon. preached before the House of Commons. May 12, 1646, being the day of their solemn thanksgiving for regaining and taking in the. garrisons of the City of Exeter, Barnstaple, etc." Published in 1646.

1661

Blake, Martin: Born in 1594 and died in 1673, authored "An earnest plea for peace and moderation : in a sermon preached at Barnstaple in Devon, to the ministers and others occasionally there assembled, Octob. 17, 1660." Publisher: printed for Francis Eglesfield (London). Published in 1661.

1680

Publication: Publication of "The Case concerning the election of Barnstaple, Devon." Published in 1680.

1698

Brewster, Francis, Sir: Publication of "A discourse concerning Ireland and the different interests thereof in answer to the Exon and Barnstaple petitions: shewing that if a law were enacted to prevent the exportation of woollen-manufactures from Ireland to foreign parts, what the consequences thereof would be both to England and Ireland." Publisher: printed for Tho. Nott and are to be sold by E. Whitlock (London). Published in 1698.

1711

Deloney, Thomas: Born in 1543 and died in 1600, authored "The lamentation of Mr. Page's wife of Plymouth : who being forced to wed him, consented to his murder, for the love of Mr. George Strangwidge, for which they suffer'd death at Barnstaple in Devonshire. To the tune of, Fortune my foe, etc. (Lamentation of Mr. Pages wife of Plimouth) (Mrs. Page's complaint for causing her husband to be murthered for the love of Mr. George Strangwidge) (Mr. George Strangwidge's lamentation for consenting to Mr. Page's death)." Publisher: printed and sold by John White (Newcastle upon Tyne). Published in 1711-1769.

1732

Squire, Francis: Born in 1682 and died in 1750, authored "The west country farmer, (number 2,) consisting of three parts: I. The landlord's answer to his tenant's complaint,. II. The farmer's reply,. III. A postscript to the farmers themselves,." Publisher: printed and sold by W. Norris, for the author: sold by Mr. Raikes in Gloucester, Mr. Wilson and Mr. Brown in Bristol, Mr. Tozer in Exon, Mr. Shute in Tiverton, and Mr. Gaydon, jun. in Barnstaple (Taunton). Published in 1732.

1734

Lucke, Robert: Born in 1674 and died in 1749, authored "The orphans legacy. A sermon preach'd in the parish-church of Barnstaple, on Sunday, May 5, 1734, occasion'd by the death of the Rev. Mr. Samuel Thompson,. By R. Luck,." Publisher: printed at Exon by E. Farley, and sold by J. Gaydon, in Barnstaple (Exeter). Published in 1734.

1743

Hole, Archdeacon of Barnstaple, etc. William: Publication of "A sermon (on Haggai i. 8) preached in the Parish-Church of Warrington, Devon, at the consecration of that Church,. Sept. 7, 1743." Published in 1743.

1752

Southcomb, Lewis: Born in 1555 and died in 1632, authored "The Christian's peculiar character: or, universal love the truest mark of a Christian.. A sermon, preach'd at Trinity-Chapel, by Honiton House, in Southmolton, Devon, on January the 1st, being the first day of the new calculation,. By Lewis Southcomb, ..." Publisher: printed and sold by R. Goadby; the booksellers of Exeter, Tiverton, and Barnstaple; Mr. Nankivell, in St. Austle; and Mr. Allison, in Falmouth (Sherborne). Published in 1752.

1753

Elworthy, John: Born in 1713 and died in 1794, authored "The influences of the spirit, and their uses, consider'd: a sermon, preached at the visitation of. George, Lord Bishop of Exeter, held at Barnstaple, July the 9th, 1753. By John Elworthy, ." Publisher: printed for Edward Score; and sold by Samuel Birt, in London, James Fletcher, in Oxford, and Benj. Matthews, in Bath (Exon). Published in 1753.

1756

Publication: Publication of "Divine alarms and warnings to a sinful people considered and improved elektronisk materiale a sermon preached at Barnstaple, in the county of Devon, on February 6. 1756. Being the day appointed for a general fasting and humiliation. By Joseph Baller." Published in 1756.

1757

HMS Antelope (1741): On April 30, 1757, Captain Samuel Hood, took command of "Antelope". On May 15, after a short action off Brest, France, the French "Aquilon", 50, was driven on to the rocks in Audierne Bay where she was wrecked. Then, on October 31, 1758, off Barnstaple, "Antelope" took "Belliqueux", 64, one of a French squadron returning from Quebec. [WP]

1769

Turner, John: Author of "A sermon, occasioned by the death of the Rev. Mr John Rutter. Preached at Honiton, May 14, 1769. By John Turner." Publisher: printed by R. Trewman, for Arthur Brown, in Honiton; sold also by R. Baldwin, London; E. Score, in Exeter; R. Goadby, in Sherborne; J. Wallis, and R. Haydon, in Plymouth; J. Fursman, in Ashburton; M. Allison, in Falmouth; F. Murch, in Barnstaple; J. Trownson, and W. Cleave, in Totness (Exeter). Published in 1769.

1778

Hardy, James of Barnstaple: Author of "A candid examination of what has been advanced on the colic of Poitou and Devonshire, with remarks on the most probable, and experiments intended to ascertain the true causes of the gout." Published in 1778.

1785

Carwithen, William. pre: Born in 1751 and died in 1824, authored "The seasons of life. A poem. In four parts. By the Rev. William Carwithen, A.B." Publisher: printed for the author by R. Trewman; sold also by G. and T. Wilkie, London; R. Crutwell, Bath; M. Haydon and Son, Plymouth; F. Murch, Barnstaple; and all other booksellers in town and country (Exeter). Published in 1785.

1795

Parkin, James: Author of "A sermon preached at Chumleigh, May 7, 1793. At the visitation of the Rev. the Archdeacon of Barnstaple. By James Parkin,." Publisher: printed and sold by B. Law and Son; Trueman and Son, Exeter; and J. Hewett, Penzance (London). Published in 1795.

1797

Donoghue, J.: Author of "Juvenile essays in poetry. By J. Donoghue." Publisher: Syle, printer, Barnstaple. Sold by L.B. Seeley, and J. Owen, London (Barnstaple). Published in 1797.

Mellen, Pastor of the East Church in Barnstaple, Mass. John.: Publication of "A Sermon (on 1 Pet. ii. 15) delivered before the. Governor, and the. Legislature of. Massachusetts, on the annual election, etc." Published in 1797.

1798

Wilson, M.P. for Barnstaple. Richard: Publication of "A letter to. Lord Loughborough, Lord High Chancellor of England, etc. from R. W. on the subject of his bill of divorce from the Hon. A. Wilson, etc." Published in 1798.

1799

Mellen, Pastor of the East Church in Barnstaple, Mass. John.: Publication of "A Discourse (on Acts xvii. 27) on natural religion, delivered in the Chapel of Harvard University in Cambridge,. at the Lecture founded by the Hon. P. Dudley." Published in 1799.

1802

B., T.: Publication of "A Dialogue, between the Old Squire Squib and a Worthy Freeman of Barnstaple, in London. (In verse. Signed: T. B., i.e. T. Billinger.)." Published in 1802.

1806

Randall, of Barnstaple. J.: Author of "The Dapiad. A mock heroic poem, in six cantos." Published in 1806.

Taprell, Richard: Author of "Barnstaple. A poem." Published in 1806.

Wilson, M.P. for Barnstaple. Richard: Publication of "A Correspondence between R. W.,. the Rt. Hon. W. Elliot,. and the Rt. Hon. G. Ponsonby, Lord High Chancellor of Ireland; relative to the persecutions of the Roman Catholics in his district by a certain description of Orangemen, etc." Published in 1806.

1807

Wilson, Richard, M. P. for Barnstaple: Publication of "A correspondence between Richard Wilson, esq. a magistrate for the county of Tyrone, and late member of the British Parliament; The Rt. Hon. George Ponsonby, lord high chancellor of Ireland: relative to the persecutions of the Roman catholics in his district, by a certain description of Orangemen, and the manner in which the laws are administered, with regard to the lower class of people; with a short introduction, in which allusions are made to former communications and conversations which Mr. Wilson had with Mr. Windham, Lord Eldon, Mr. Wickham, and Sir Evan Nepean, upon the above-mentioned subjects." Published in 1807.

1808

Wilson, M.P. for Barnstaple. Richard: Publication of "A narrative of various murders and robberies, committed in the neighbourhood of the relater, upon the Roman Catholics, by a banditti describing themselves Orangemen; with his letters to the Duke of Richmond, and Lord Manners, etc." Published in 1808.

1809

Rodd Point, New South Wales: Rodd Point is named after the Rodd family who contributed to the area for almost a century, and includes land bought by Brent Clements Rodd (1809-1898) from the Five Dock Farm estate in 1836. Rodd had a large family of 12 children and many of the local streets are named after members of the Rodd family: Brent, Brisbane, Burnell, Clements, Janet, Lenore, Rodd, Trevanion and Undine. Barnstaple Road takes its name from Barnstaple Manor, Rodd's family home which in turn took its name from his birthplace in Britain. [WP]

1811

Gardiner, H. W.: Author of "A collection of hymns, from various authors, intended as a supplement to the psalms and hymns of Dr. Watts, and Dr. Doddridge. By H.W. Gardiner." Publisher: printed by J. Avery (Barnstaple). Published in 1811.

1815

Publication: Publication of "Completion of the road to the Lands End with roads to Dartmouth Plymouth, Fowey, Falmouth, Padstow, Biddeford and Barnstaple. (map)." Publisher: published by Laurie & Whittle London., 12th Feb (London). Published in 1815.

1816

Randall, John, of Barnstaple: Publication of "An address to the electors of the United Kingdom in general, and the borough of Barnstaple in particular: with hints for candidates." Publisher: printed for the author, and sold by Simpkin and Marshall (London). Published in 1816.

Townsend, John Haynes: Born in 1779 and died in 1865, authored "A call to unanimity in the Established Church." Publisher: printed by W. Syle, for J Hatchard (Barnstaple). Published in 1816.

1818

Austin, W. I.: Author of "Sermons, on various subjects." By the Rev. W. I. Austin. Publisher: J. Avery (Barnstaple). Published in 1818.

1819

Great Britain. Parliament. House of Commons Select Committee on the Barnstaple Election: Publication of "Report from the Select Committee on the Barnstaple Election: together with the special report from the said Committee, and also the minutes of evidence taken before them: ordered, by the House of Commons, to be printed, 9 March 1819." Published in 1819.

Publication: Publication of "Remarks upon a bill for altering the right of voting for members of Parliament, for the borough of Barnstaple." Publisher: printed by J. Haddon (London). Published in 1819.

1820

Publication: Publication of "Elementary thoughts on the bullion question, the national debt, the resources of Great Britain, and the probable duration of the constitution." Publisher: printed by J. Avery (Barnstaple). Published in 1820.

1823

Publication: Publication of "The Barnstaple miscellany." Published in 1823.

1824

PERIODICAL PUBLICATIONS. Barnstaple: Publication of "The North Devon Magazine; containing the Cave and Lundy Review." Published in 1824.

Publication: Publication of "The North Devon magazine." Publisher: W. Searle (Barnstaple (Devon, England)). Published in 1824.

1827

Alexander Henry Haliday: Thomas Ansell Marshall (1827-1903) The College Milford Haven later Barnstaple Devon England Hymenoptera. [WP]

1828

Gardiner, H. W.: Author of "A cursory view of the lives of Rev. Jonathan Hanmer and the Rev. John Hanmer with in seven familiar letters to Thomas Welman of Poundisford Park, near Taunton." Publisher: printed and sold by J. Avery (Barnstaple). Published in 1828.

1830

Gribble, Joseph Besly: Author of "Memorials of Barnstaple; being an attempt to supply the want of a history of that ancient borough. By Joseph Besly Gribble." Published in 1830.

1831

Bartholomew, Archdeacon of Barnstaple. John.: Publication of "A Sermon preached. at the Consecration of Henry, Lord Bishop of Exeter (i.e. Henry Phillpotts)." Published in 1831.

1832

Boyle, Incumbent of Holy Trinity, Barnstaple. John.: Publication of "The Truth of Christianity inferred from Agrippa's Confession to Paul. A sermon preached in the Chapel of the Asylum for Female Orphans, London, etc." Published in 1832.

Denham, Henry Mangles: Author of "Remarks and Sailing Directions relative to Lundy Island, and the north coast of Devonshire, between Hartland-Point and Combe-Martin, including the bar and ports of Barnstaple and Bideford, with Ilfracombe Harbour. By Lieut. H. M. Denham. Published to." Published in 1832.

1835

Shuttleworth, Philip Nicolas: Born in 1782 and died in 1842, authored "'The carnal mind is enmity against God': a sermon, preached in the Parish Church of Bideford, August 9, 1835, on the occasion of the annual meeting of the District Committees of the Society for Promoting Christian Knowledge, established within the Archdeaconry of Barnstaple." By the Rev. P.N. Shuttleworth, D.D. Publisher: printed for J.G. & F. Rivington (London). Published in 1835.

1836

Boyle, Incumbent of Holy Trinity, Barnstaple. John.: Publication of "Sermons on some Leading Points of Christian Doctrine and Duty." Published in 1836.

Five Dock, New South Wales: The earliest local roads were developed by the auctioneer Samuel Lyons, who purchased "Five Dock Farm" from Harris in 1836. "Lyons Road" bears his surname today. Lyons soon subdivided the land into 133 lots and sold them at auction. These were 12-24 hectare blocks of land and were generally used for large country-style residences such as Barnstaple Manor. [WP]

1837

England, Churches and Religious Bodies: Publication of "Report of the District Committees of the Society. established within the Archdeaconry of Barnstaple, 1837." Published in 1837.

1841

Boyle, Incumbent of Holy Trinity, Barnstaple. John.: Publication of "Reasons for preferring the Worship of the Established Church. Second edition." Published in 1841.

1843

Boyle, John, Incumbent of Holy Trinity, Barnstaple: Publication of "A plea for the Episcopal Church in Scotland, in a brief defence of the "Scotch Communion Office."." Published in 1843.

Dickinson, Robert William: Author of "Vexata quæstio: being two addresses on the depreciation of the currency, delivered at Barnstaple on the 3rd day of February and the 3rd day of March, 1843." Publisher: J. Clarke (London). Published in 1843.

1844

Avery, John G., ed: Publication of "Memorials of the Rev. John Henley." Compiled by his widow and edited by John G. Avery. Publisher: W. Avery (Barnstaple, England). Published in 1844.

Boyle, Incumbent of Holy Trinity, Barnstaple. John.: Publication of "Poetry and Prose. A collection of original compositions contributed for the benefit of a fund raised for Church purposes By C. G. S. and others. Edited by the Reverend J. Boyle." Published in 1844.

Francis Carruthers Gould: Francis Carruthers Gould (December 2, 1844 - 1925), English caricaturist and politician, was born in Barnstaple. [WP]

W. Avery: Publisher of "Memorials of the Rev. John Henley." Compiled by his widow and edited by John G. Avery. Publisher: W. Avery (Barnstaple, England). Published in 1844.

1845

Barnstaple, Barnstaple Literary and Scientific Institution: Publication of "Rules and Regulations, etc." Published in 1845.

1847

Soltau, G. W.: Author of "Trout flies of Devon and Cornwall, and when and how to use them." Publisher: Edward Nettleton, ((London): Longman; Exeter: Wallis and Holden; Barnstaple,: Brightwell;; Bodmin: Liddell; Truro: Heard and Sons; Plymouth). Published in 1847.

William Fraser: He was educated at Eton and at Christ Church, Oxford, entered the 1st Life Guards in 1847, but retired with a captain's rank in 1852. He then set about entering parliament, and the ups and downs of his political career were rather remarkable. He was returned for Barnstaple in 1852, but the election was declared void on account of bribery, and the constituency was disfranchised for two years. [WP]

1850

Bartholomew, Archdeacon of Barnstaple. John.: Publication of "The Aggressive Character of the Church of Rome. A sermon, etc." Published in 1850.

Wrey Henry B.: Publication of "A sermon preached in the Parish Church of Tawstock, Devon, on the fifth day of November, 1850." By the Reverend Henry B. Wrey. Publisher: W. Searle (Barnstaple). Published in 1850.

1851

William Tite: Tite's active work ceased about twenty years before his death. In 1851 he visited Italy after a grave illness. In 1854 he contested Barnstaple unsuccessfully as a Liberal, but in the following year was returned as member of parliament for Bath, which he represented until his death. He keenly opposed Sir George Gilbert Scott's proposal to build the new Foreign and Commonwealth Office and other government buildings adjacent to HM Treasury in Whitehall in the Gothic style. In 1869 he was knighted, and in 1870 was made a Companion of the Bath. Tite had a wide knowledge of English literature and was a good linguist; he was an active citizen and a lover of old books. [WP]

1852

Bartholomew, John 1791?-1865. pre: Born in 1790 and died in 1865, authored "Convocation: A charge delivered to the clergy of the archdeaconry of Barnstaple, at the ordinary visitation, A.D.

1952." Publisher: John Henry Parker; Exeter Henry John Wallis (Oxford; London). Published in 1852.

1853

Pycroft, James: Author of "Literature compatible with a busy life: an inaugural lecture delivered by request to the Barnstaple Early Closing Association, on the 31st December 1852, and published by the author's permission." Publisher: G.J. Jenvey (Barnstaple). Published in 1853.

1855

C. W.: Publication of "A short historical sketch of the town of Barnstaple, etc." The preface signed: C.W. Published in 1855.

1858

Bartholomew, John, Archdeacon of Barnstaple: Publication of "A charge delivered to the clergy of the Archdeaconry of Barnstaple, at his visitation, in June, 1858." Published in 1858.

Boyle, John, Incumbent of Holy Trinity, Barnstaple: Publication of "How and for what we ought to pray: a series of lectures on the Lord's Prayer; with reasons for preferring the worship of the established church." Published in 1858.

1859

Barnstaple: Publication of "A list of the voters who polled at the election of members to serve in Parliament for the borough of Barnstaple, on the 30th of April, 1859." Published in 1859.

William Fraser: At the election of 1857 Sir William, who had meantime been defeated at Harwich, was again returned at Barnstaple. He was, defeated in 1859, but was elected in 1863 at Ludlow. This seat he held for only two years, when he was again defeated and did not re-enter parliament until 1874, when he was returned for Kidderminster, a constituency he represented for six years, when be retired. He was a familiar figure at the Carlton Club, always ready with a copious collection of anecdotes of Wellington, Disraeli and Napoleon III. [WP]

1860

Bartholomew, John 1791?-1865. pre: Publication of "The census and the church rate: a charge delivered by the Venerable the Archdeacon of Barnstaple." Published in 1860.

Boyle, John, Incumbent of Holy Trinity, Barnstaple: Publication of "The sacrament of the body and blood of Christ, doctrinally and practically explained." Published in 1860.

Neale, W. R.: Author of "Time the avenger and other poems." Publisher: W. Kent & Co., Barnstaple: Cornish (London). Published in 1860.

Pinder, Humphrey Senhouse, M. A., Rector of Bratton-Fleming, Barnstaple: Author of "A plea for country bishops: in a letter to a friend." Publisher: Joseph Masters (London). Published in 1860.

Yates, John, of Barnstaple: Publication of "An essay on manufactured cattle foods." Published in 1860.

1862

Addison, Edward: Born in 1820 and died in 1861, authored "Sermons preached on various occasions." By the late Rev. Edward Addison, formerly missionary to western Africa, carefully transcribed from posthumous manuscripts; with a brief memoir. Publisher: printed and published by J.G Hayman, 'North Devon Journal' Office (Barnstaple). Published in 1862.

Sadler, Vicar of Coleridge. William: Publication of "God's Claims to our Love. A sermon (on Luke x. 27) preached at the visitation of. the Archdeacon of Barnstaple in the Parish Church of Southmolton, on June 17, 1862, etc." Published in 1862.

UNITED STATES OF AMERICA. Departments of State and Public Institutions: Publication of "Cape Cod Ship Canal. Report of the Advisory Council of the Joint Committee of the Massachusetts Legislature on a Ship Canal to connect Barnstaple Bay and Buzzard's Bay."

Published in 1862.

1863

Bartholomew, Archdeacon of Barnstaple. John.: Publication of "Choral Association. A sermon preached. at the first meeting of the Choral Association for the Archdeaconry of Barnstaple." Published in 1863.

1864

Bartholomew, John, Archdeacon of Barnstaple: Publication of "Choral association, a sermon preached June 15, 1864, at the meeting of the Choral association for the archdeaconry of Barnstable." Published in 1864.

1865

Chanter, John Roberts: Author of "Sketches of some Striking Incidents in the History of Barnstaple, being the substance of a lecture, etc." Published in 1865.

Maclowman, Alexander: Author of "Rambles around Barnstaple, in the year 1865. By A. M. L. i.e. Alexander McLowman." Published in 1865.

Newnam, Samuel: Author of "Lectures, delivered in the Music Hall, Barnstaple. 1857-8." Published in 1865.

1866

Chanter, John Roberts: Author of "Sketches of the literary history of Barnstaple, being the substance of a series of papers read at the Literary institution, Barnstaple, by John Roberts Chanter, to which is appended the diary of Philip Wyot, town clerk of Barnstaple, from 1586 to 1608." Publisher: printed and sold by E.J. Arnold pref (Barnstaple). Published in 1866.

Hole, Charles Henry, M. A., Curate of Barnstaple: Publication of "A Greek primer." Published in 1866.

Woollcombe, Henry: Author of "A Charge delivered at the first visitation of the Archdeaconry of Barnstaple, on May 14th, 15th, 16th, 18th, 1866." Published in 1866.

1869

Bain, Joseph: Born in 1826 and died in 1911, authored "Letter: 1869 Feb. 22, Lynmouth, Barnstaple, to David Laing." Published in 1869.

1870

Bain, Joseph: Born in 1826 and died in 1911, authored "Letter: 1870 Mar. 30, Rock Lodge, Lynmouth, Barnstaple, to David Laing." Published in 1870.

Bertram, Robert Aitken: Born in 1836 and died in 1886, authored "The love of God to man. A sermon preached in the Music Hall, Barnstaple, on Sunday, the 17th of April, 1870." Published in 1870.

1871

Bain, Joseph: Born in 1826 and died in 1911, authored "Letter: 1871 May 15, Rock Lodge, Lynton, Barnstaple, to David Laing." Published in 1871.

Brereton, Prebendary of Exeter Cathedral. Joseph Lloyd: Publication of "School Boards. An address to the Barnstaple Farmers' Club." Published in 1871.

1872

Bain, Joseph: Born in 1826 and died in 1911, authored "Letter: 1872 Aug. 21, Rock Lodge, Lynton, Barnstaple, to David Laing." Published in 1872.

Bertram, Robert Aitken: Born in 1836 and died in 1886, authored "Co-workers with God. A sermon to Sunday school teachers, preached in the Congregational Chapel Barnstaple, June 9th, 1872." Published in 1872.

Brereton, Prebendary of Exeter Cathedral. Joseph Lloyd: Publication of "County Endowments. An address to the Barnstaple Farmers' Club." Published in 1872.

Robert Louis Stevenson Quotation: "The Scene

is laid in the neighbourhood of Barnstaple." - Robert Louis Stevenson in Plays of Henley and R.L. Stevenson.

1873

Bain, Joseph: Born in 1826 and died in 1911, authored "Letter: 1873 Nov. 5, Lynton, Barnstaple, to David Laing." Published in 1873.

Hobbs, J. J.: Author of "God's retributive judgments: a letter to Mr R.C., of Barnstaple." By J.J. Hobbs, Blandford. Publisher: printed by C. Doe (Yeovil). Published in 1873.

1874

Bain, Joseph: Born in 1826 and died in 1911, authored "Letter: 1874 Feb. 14, Rock Lodge, Lynton, Barnstaple, to David Laing." Published in 1874.

Bertram, Robert Aitkin: Author of "Children in the market-place: a farewell sermon, preached in Cross St. Chapel, Barnstaple, Sept. 27th, 1874." Published in 1874.

Samuel Danks Waddy: Samuel Danks Waddy (1830-1902) was an English politician. He was born in Gateshead, the son of Richard Waddy a Methodist minister. He moved to Sheffield with his family when his father was appointed as the Head Master of the new Wesley College (now King Edward VII School). He was elected as the Liberal Member of Parliament M.P. for Barnstaple, Devon on 3 February 1874 but resigned this seat in December 1879 to stand in a by-election in the Sheffield constituency, taking the seat on 21 December 1879. However he held the Sheffield seat for less than four months, being voted out by just 40 votes on 3 April 1880. He was elected to Edinburgh in 1882, and when that seat was abolished, he contested, but lost, the new Hallam seat in 1885. He was elected as M.P. for Brigg, Lincolnshire on 7 July 1886, a seat he held until 1894 when he was appointed Recorder of Sheffield. In 1896 he was appointed as Judge of the Cheshire County Court but only held the position for two weeks, transferring to be Judge of the Sheffield County Court on 24 April 1896. [WP]

1878

Russell, Perpetual Curate of Swymbridge, Barnstaple. John.: Publication of "A Memoir of the Rev. J. Russell, and his out-of-door life. By the author of 'Dartmoor Days,' etc. Edward W. L. Davies. With illustrations." Published in 1878.

1881

Temple, Frederick abp. of Canterbury. pre: Publication of "Charge, delivered at the visitation of the archdeaconry of Barnstaple, by Frederick, lord bishop of Exeter." Published in 1881.

1882

Chanter, John Roberts: Author of "Memorials, descriptive and historical, of the Church of St. Peter, Barnstaple, with its other ecclesiastical antiquities, and an account of the Conventual Church of St. Mary Magdalene, etc." Published in 1882.

1886

Barnstaple: Publication of "Guide Book to Barnstaple, Ilfracombe and North Devon.(Revised edition.)." Published in 1886.

1887

Ward, Lock and Co: Author of "Ward and Lock's historical and pictorial guide to Ilfracombe, Barnstaple and the North-West of Devonshire. With maps and engravings." Published in 1887.

1888

Barnstaple, North Devon Athenæum: Publication of "Rules of the North Devon Athenæum. 1888." Published in 1888.

1889

Cotton, Richard William: Author of "Barnstaple and the Northern Part of Devonshire during the Great Civil War, 1642-1646." Published in 1889.

Publication: Publication of "(Ordnance Plan of the Town of Barnstaple. Scale, 1: 500 or 10·56 feet= 1 mile)." Published in 1889.

1895

George Moore Quotation: "Many changes were taking place in Barnstaple, new houses were being built, a much larger and finer shop had been opened in the more prosperous end of the town, and Mrs. Waters found herself obliged to sell her business for almost nothing, and marry again." - George Moore in Esther Waters.

George Moore Quotation: "I was brought up by the seaside at Barnstaple. On the beach I met Mrs. Leopold, that is to say Mrs. Randal, John's wife; she seemed to be in great trouble, she looked that melancholy, and for company's sake she asked me to come home to tea with her." - George Moore in Esther Waters.

George Moore Quotation: "They had left Barnstaple many months, and were now living in a little street off the Vauxhall Bridge Road, near the factory where Saunders worked; and since they had been in London Esther had been constantly in service." - George Moore in Esther Waters.

George Moore Quotation: "She loved to expatiate on her inexhaustible affection for dumb animals, and she continued an anecdotal discourse till, suddenly wearying of it, she would break off and speak to Esther about Barnstaple and the Brethren." - George Moore in Esther Waters.

George Moore Quotation: "Esther Waters came from Barnstaple." - George Moore in Esther Waters.

Great Britain: Publication of "An act for making a railway between Barnstaple and Lynton in the County of Devon and for other purposes: (27th June 1895)." Publisher: printed by Eyre and Spottiswoode (London). Published in 1895.

Industries: Publication of "Industries of west England business review. An illustrated, historical and commercial guide to Ilfracombe, Barnstaple, Bideford. and district. Manufacturers and merchants." Published in 1895.

Lynton and Barnstaple Railway: Following the opening of the Devon & Somerset Railway to Barnstaple, there were calls for the railway to be extended to serve the twin villages of Lynton and Lynmouth which were popular with holiday-makers. Because of the difficult nature of the terrain it was decided to economise by using the two-foot gauge (actually one foot 11.5 inches), as already used on the Festiniog Railway and elsewhere. The scheme was supported by Sir George Newnes who became chairman of the railway company. The Lynton & Barnstaple Railway Bill was passed by the United Kingdom Parliament on 27th June 1895, and the first train ran on 11th May 1898. [WP]

1897

Gardiner, William Francis: Author of "Barnstaple, 1837-1897." Publisher: Allan (Barnstaple). Published in 1897.

Pennell, Joseph: Author of the image "Barnstaple." Published in 1897.

1898

Napier, Arthur Sampson: Born in 1853 and died in 1916, authored "On Barnstaple as a mintina-place." By Prof Arthur S. Napier and Sir John Evans. Publisher: Numismatic Chronicle (London). Published in 1898.

WARD, LOCK AND CO.: Publication of "A New Pictorial and Descriptive Guide to Ilfracombe, Barnstaple, and North-West Devon. Illustrations, etc." Published in 1898.

1900

A. E. Barnes: Publisher of "Reprint of the Barnstaple Records, published by J. R. Chanter and Thos. Wainwright. With corrections and additions by Thos. Wainwright." Publisher: A. E. Barnes (Barnstaple). Published in 1900.

Barnstaple: Publication of "Reprint of the

Barnstaple Records, published by J. R. Chanter and Thos. Wainwright. With corrections and additions by Thos. Wainwright." Published in 1900.

Publication: Publication of "Reprint of the Barnstaple records." (edited by) John Roberts Chanter and Thomas Wainwright. Published in 1900.

1901

Francis Chichester: Sir Francis Chichester, aviator and sailor, (born September 17, 1901, Barnstaple, Devon, England - died August 26, 1972, Plymouth, Devon) was knighted by Queen Elizabeth II for his achievement of sailing solo around the world in only nine months and one day. [WP]

1902

Bennet, W. H.: Author of "Robert Cleaver Chapman of Barnstaple, etc (Illustrated.)." Publisher: Pickering & Inglis, (Glasgow). Published in 1902.

1903

Barnstaple: Publication of "Barnstaple Parish Register of Baptisms Marriages and Burials, 1538 A.D. to 1812 A.D. Edited by Thos. Wainwright." Published in 1903.

J. G. Commin: Publisher of "Barnstaple Parish Register of Baptisms Marriages and Burials, 1538 A.D. to 1812 A.D. Edited by Thos. Wainwright." Publisher: J. G. Commin (Exeter). Published in 1903.

James G. Commin: Publisher of "Barnstaple parish register, 1538 A.D. to 1812 A.D.." Publisher: James G. Commin (Exeter). Published in 1903.

1904

Gardiner, William Francis: Author of "Mate's Illustrated Barnstaple, past and present, etc." Published in 1904.

PERIODICAL PUBLICATIONS. Barnstaple: Publication of "Action for Libel against the North Devon Herald heard at Exeter on February 2nd, 1904. Reprint of portion of the proceedings." Published in 1904.

1907

Ephemerides: Publication of "Shepperd's Barnstaple Almanack." Published in 1907.

Gardiner, William Francis: Author of "The Official Guide to Barnstaple, etc." Published in 1907.

1909

Inch, Maude Elizabeth: Author of "'A Nautical Knot' or 'The Belle of Barnstaple.' Operetta in two acts. Books and lyrics by M. E. Inch. Music by Wm. Rhys-Herbert. Words only." Published in 1909.

1910

Chanter, John Frederick: Author of "The life and times of Martin Blake 1593-1673, vicar of Barnstaple and prebendary of Exeter Cathedral. With some account of his conflicts with the Puritan lecturers and persecutions. (With plates.)." Published in 1910.

1911

CRESSWELL, Beatrix Feodore: Author of "(Barnstaple and the Beauties of North Devon. A handbook for visitors and residents. Illustrated with photographs, etc. (The Corporation's official guide.) (With a map and a plan.))." Publisher: Frederick Warne & Co ((London): Homeland Association; London, New York). Published in 1911.

1912

Barnstaple, Barnstaple Grammar School: Publication of "Barnstaple Grammar School Magazine. vol. 1. no. 1." Published in 1912.

1914

Barnstaple: Publication of "Historical Pageant of Old Barnstaple. Five scenes performed in the Theatre Royal, at Barnstaple, on Wednesday, January 28th, 1914. Edited by R. J. E. Boggis." Published in 1914.

1915

Boggis, Robert James Edmund: Publication of "A History of the Parish and Church of St. Mary Magdalene, Barnstaple." Published in 1915.

Eliot, John: Born in 1604 and died in 1690, authored "John Eliot and the Indians, 1652-1657: being letters addressed to Rev. Johnathan Hanmer of Barnstaple..." Publisher: The Adams & Grace press (New York). Published in 1915.

1917

Reichel, Oswald Joseph: Author of "Barnstaple and its three Sub-manors, part of the inland hundred of Braunton. Reprinted from the Transactions of the Devonshire Association for the Advancement of Science. 1917." Published in 1917.

1923

London and South Western Railway: The London and South Western Railway (L&SWR) was a railway company in the England from 1840 to 1923. Its ultimate network extended from London to Plymouth via Yeovil, Exeter and Okehampton with branches to Barnstaple and Wadebridge - a territory in which it was in direct competition with the Great Western Railway - and, via Basingstoke, Winchester and Southampton, along the Dorset coast to Bournemouth and Weymouth. It also had a large number of branches which connected to places such as Portsmouth. Following the grouping in 1923, the L&SWR lines became part of the Southern Railway. [WP]

Lynton and Barnstaple Railway: In 1923 the railway became part of the Southern Railway. In 1925 a fifth locomotive, "Lew" was purchased, built to a design based on the Manning Wardle originals. [WP]

1924

Ward, Lock: Publisher of "A pictorial and descriptive guide to Barnstaple, Ilfracombe, Bideford, Clovelly and north-west Devon." Publisher: Ward, Lock (London). Published in 1924.

1925

Edwards, Henry John: Author of "Roses in the Snow. A Christmas Carol, words by V. D. Tennyson, etc." Publisher: The Composer (Barnstaple). Published in 1925.

1926

Corporation: Publication of "Official Guide and Souvenir to Barnstaple. Published by authority of the Barnstaple Corporation. (With a map.)." Publisher: british Publishing Co (Gloucester). Published in 1926.

Wells, Herbert George: Born in 1866 and died in 1946, authored "M. Barnstaple chez les hommes-dieux: roman." Traduit de l'anglais par Louis Labat. Published in 1926.

WRIGHT, Frederick Robert Elliston: Author of "Braunton. A few nature notes. With lists of flora, macro lepidoptera and birds known to occur in the district. (With plates and a map.)." Publisher: A. E. Barnes (Barnstaple). Published in 1926.

1930

Barnstaple: Publication of "The borough of a thousand years, 930-1930. Being the official millenary souvenir brochure." Published in 1930.

WARD, LOCK AND CO.: Publication of "Barnstaple. A Pictorial and Descriptive Guide to Barnstaple, Ilfracombe, Bideford, Clovelly and Northwest Devon. Eleventh, etc. edition, revised. With maps." Published in 1930.

1933

Noyes, Edward MacArthur: Author of "Sermon preached at West Barnstaple, Mass., Henry Jacob Sunday, Aug. 6, 1933." Published in 1933.

1938

Barnstaple: Publication of "Barnstaple. The official guide and souvenir. Editor, H. G. W. McWhinnie.With illustrations." Published in 1938.

1940

Drake, Daphne: Author of "Members of Parliament for Barnstaple; 1492-1688, 1689-1832: (&) Additions & corrections. (Transactions of the Devonshire Association for the advancement of science, literature and art.)." Published in 1940.

1941

Mark Bonham Carter: Educated at Winchester College and Balliol College, Oxford, where he read PPE, his studies were interrupted by the Second World War, and was commissioned in the Grenadier Guards in 1941. Captured in Tunisia in 1943 and imprisoned in Italy, he escaped and walked four hundred miles to return to British lines, being mentioned in despatches. Bonham Carter concluded the war by standing as the unsuccessful Liberal candidate for Barnstaple in the 1945 general election, before returning to finish the last year of his course at Oxford. He then spent a year at the University of Chicago before going into publishing, working for the Collins publishing firm. [WP]

1942

Freemasons England, order of roy. arch masons: Publication of "By-laws of the Royal arch chapter of loyalty and virtue, no. 251, formerly no. 469, Barnstaple." Published in 1942.

1946

Box, Frank E.: Author of "Gradients. Barnstaple and Ilfracombe Branch, Southern Railway." Published in 1946.

1947

Barnstaple, Rural District of.: Publication of "The Official Guide to Barnstaple Rural District. With. map and. illustrations." Published in 1947.

Ward, Lock and Co: Author of "A pictorial and descriptive guide to Barnstaple, Ilfracombe, Bideford, Clovelly and North-West Devon maps and plans illustrations." Published in 1947.

1948

Barnstaple, Rural District of. Council: Publication of "North Devon. The Offical Guide of the Barnstaple Rural District Council. Second (-Fifth) edition." Published in 1948.

Elliott, F. C.: Author of "Around Barnstaple. With plates." Published in 1948.

1949

Barnstaple: Publication of "Barnstaple. The official guide.With maps and illustrations." Published in 1949.

Catchpole, Leslie Thomas: Author of "The Lynton & Barnstaple Railway. (Fourth edition.)." Published in 1949.

1951

Publication: Publication of "Barnstaple. The official guide. (With illustrations.)." Published in 1951.

Ward, Lock and Co: Author of "Guide to Ilfracombe, Barnstaple, Bideford, Woolacombe, Clovelly and North-West Devon, etc." Published in 1951.

1954

Catchpole, L. T.: Author of "The Lynton &

Barnstaple railway." Publisher: Oakwood Press (South Godstone, Surrey). Published in 1954.

1956

Barnstaple, Rural District of. Council: Publication of "North Devon. The official guide to Barnstaple Rural District Council. Illustrated. With a map." Published in 1956.

Holmes, Frank: Author of "Brother indeed. (The life of Robert Cleaver Chapman, 'Barnstaple patriarch.') With plates, including portraits." Published in 1956.

1960

Brown, Gordon Arthur: Author of "The Operation of the Lynton & Barnstaple Railway, 1898 to 1935. With illustrations." Published in 1960.

Directories: Publication of "Barnstaple & District Directory." Published in 1960.

1962

Bell, Leslie E.: Author of "Barnstaple. Street map." (projection drawn by Leslie E. Bell). Publisher: Taw-Vale Duplicating (Barnstaple). Published in 1962.

1963

WARD, LOCK AND CO.: Publication of "Devon, North-West. North-West Devon. Ilfracombe, Woolacombe, Barnstaple, Bideford, Westward Ho!, Clovelly. With plates and maps." Published in 1963.

1964

Brown, Gordon Arthur: Author of "The Lynton and Barnstaple Railway. By G. A. Brown, J. D. C. A. Prideaux, H. G. Radcliffe. With plates and maps." Published in 1964.

1965

Bell, Leslie E.: Author of "Barnstaple and around. (Street map, street index and notes.)." Published in 1965.

Mosdell, Gerald William: Author of "The Bugle. A Barnstaple broadside. Edited by G. W. Mosdell and D. Rogers; designed by S. M. Mosdell. Linocuts by P. A. Davey and S. M. Mosdell." Published in 1965.

1966

Devonshire: Publication of "Barnstaple feasibility study." Publisher: Devonshire Planning Department (Exeter). Published in 1966.

Ward, Lock and Co: Author of "Bideford and North-West Devon, Clovelly, Westward, Ho!, Barnstaple, Croyde, Woolacombe, Ilfracombe. (With plates, illustrations, maps and plans.)." Published in 1966.

1967

Porcupines: Publisher of "The bugle." Publisher: Porcupines (Barnstaple). Published in 1967.

Royal Automobile Club: Publication of "What to see in Barnstaple, Bude and Ilfracombe and the surrounding country. (With illustrations and maps.)." Published in 1967.

1968

Rogers, David James: Author of "Coarse fishing in the Barnstaple area." By D. J Rogers and G. W. Mosdell. Published in 1968.

1969

Barnstaple, Barnstaple and District Chamber of Commerce: Publication of "Barnstaple Centre for North Devon. (Official guide.. Year 1969/70.)." Published in 1969.

Common Wealth: Publication of "We hold these truths: a manifesto for libertarians." Publisher: Common Wealth (Barnstaple, (Devon)). Published in 1969.

Publication: Publication of "Barnstaple centre for North Devon." Published in 1969.

1970

Chapple, William: Born in 1718 and died in 1781, authored "Review of part of Risdon's Survey of Devon containing the general description of that county; with corrections, annotations, and additions." By the late William Chapple. Publisher: reprinted by Porcupines (Barnstaple). Published in 1970.

David & Charles: Publisher of "One-inch Ordnance Survey of England and Wales Sheet 74, Barnstaple & Lundy Island (cartographic material)." Publisher: David & Charles (Newton Abbot). Published in 1970.

Fraser, Robert: Author of "General view of the County of Devon, with observations on the means of its improvement: drawn up for the consideration of the Board of Agriculture and Internal Improvement." Publisher: Porcupines (Barnstaple). Published in 1970.

G.W. May Ltd.,: Publisher of "Barnstaple and District. (Street plan)." Publisher: G.W. May Ltd., (London). Published in 1970.

Risdon, Tristram: Born in 1580 and died in 1640, authored "The chorographical description or survey of the county of Devon: printed from a genuine copy of the original manuscript, with considerable additions." London, Printed for Rees and Curtis Plymouth, 1811. Publisher: Porcupines (Barnstaple). Published in 1970.

1971

Britain, Great: Author of "Service time tables printed for the use of the Company's servants. Bristol to Exeter, including the Weston-Super-Mare loop line and the Portishead, Clevedon, Wells, Yeovil, Chard, Minehead, Barnstaple, Tiverton, Culm Valley, Crediton, and Exe Valley bran." Publisher: Town and Country Press (Bracknell). Published in 1971.

Brown, Gordon Arthur Prideaux, J. D. C. A. jt. auth. Radcliffe, H. G. jt. auth: Publication of "The Lynton & Barnstaple Railway." By G. A. Brown, J. D. C. A. Prideaux (and) H. G. Radcliffe. Publisher: David & Charles (Newton Abbot (Eng.)). Published in 1971.

Great Britain. Treasury: Publication of "Exchequer K.R. port books 1701-1798. Part 2, South-east, South and South-West Coasts Ipswich to Barnstaple (South-east, South and South-West Coasts Ipswich to Barnstaple) (Ipswich to Barnstaple)." Publisher: Swift (London). Published in 1971.

List & Index Society: Publication of "66. Exchequer K.R. Port books, 1701-1798: part II, South and South West coasts, Ipswich to Barnstaple." Publisher: Swift Printers (London). Published in 1971.

Reed, Margaret A.: Author of "The public houses of Pilton." Publisher: Porcupines (Barnstaple (19 Pilton St., Barnstaple, Devon)). Published in 1971.

1972

Edmonds, Eric Arthur: Born in 1927, authored "The Pleistocene history of the Barnstaple area." Publisher: H.M.S.O (London). Published in 1972.

1973

Cannon, Donald V.: Author of "The history of Ashford." Publisher: D. V. Cannon, ("Glenkens", Strand La.), (Barnstaple). Published in 1973.

Devon: Publication of "Barnstaple outline plan report; report prepared jointly by the County Planning Officer and the County Surveyor, Devon County Council." Published in 1973.

1974

David and Charles: Publisher of "Lynton & Barnstaple Railway album." (compiled by) J. D. C. A. Prideaux. Publisher: David and Charles (Newton Abbot; North Pomfret, Vt.). Published in 1974.

Hill, Laura Annie Kathleen: Author of "The Old Barn, Fremington near Barnstaple L.A.K Hill." Published in 1974.

Prideaux, John Denys Charles Austice:

Publication of "Lynton & Barnstaple Railway album." Published in 1974.

Publication: Publication of "Lynton & Barnstaple Railway album (compiled by) J.D.C.A. Prideaux." Published in 1974.

1975

Glendining & Co: Publication of "English, Scottish & Irish hammered silver coins including the R.P.V. Brettell collection of coins of Barnstaple." Published in 1975.

Grant, Alison Hughes, Barry D jt. auth: Publication of "North Devon barges." By Alison Grant and Barry Hughes. Publisher: North Devon Museum Trust (Barnstaple). Published in 1975.

Harper, Richard Michael Joseph: Author of "Evolutionary origins of disease." By R. M. J Harper. Publisher: G. Mosdell (Barnstaple, (Eng.)). Published in 1975.

1976

Carrie Davies: Carrie Davies (born June 24 1976 in Barnstaple) is a sportsreader currently working for The Chris Moyles Show on BBC Radio 1 in the UK. [WP]

Lloyd, Reginald James: Author of "Paintings, drawings and monotypes in private collections." (by) R.J. Lloyd; (compiled by Louise MacMillan). Publisher: Porcupines ((Barnstaple) ((19 Pilton St., Barnstaple, Devon))). Published in 1976.

1977

Ontario Hydro. Design and Development Division Barnstaple, A. G Drewes, P. L.: Publication of "Wind power on Pelee Island." Publisher: Ontario Hydro (Ontario). Published in 1977.

1978

Baker, William Thomas: Author of "They took the lifeboat up the mountainside: the Lynmouth flood, 15th August, 1952." By William T. Baker; photographs by R.L. Knight. Publisher: The author,, (Barnstaple (12 Abbey Rd, Barnstable, Devon)). Published in 1978.

Ontario Hydro. Energy and Environmental Studies Dept Barnstaple, A. G Tong, W. S.: Publication of "Residential district heating with moderator heat from CANDU power plants." Publisher: Ontario Hydro, Design and Development Division (Toronto). Published in 1978.

Publication: Publication of "Barnstaple & district official guide." Published in 1978.

1979

Forward Publicity Ltd.,: Publisher of "Barnstaple. Official street plan." Publisher: Forward Publicity Ltd., (Wallington). Published in 1979.

Ontario Hydro. Power Equipment and Energy Studies Dept Barnstaple, A. G Drewes, P.: Publication of "Utility fuel cell power plant study." Published in 1979.

Publication: Publication of "The Lynton & Barnstaple Railway (compiled by) J.R. Yeomans." Published in 1979.

Yeomans, J. R.: Author of "The Lynton & Barnstaple Railways." (compiled by) J. R. Yeomans. Publisher: Barton (Truro). Published in 1979.

1980

H.J. Chard: Publisher of "Barnstaple yesterday: over 160 photographs of Barnstaple from the 1860's onwards." (compiled) by Julia & Jonathan Baxter. Publisher: H.J. Chard (Bristol). Published in 1980.

Hurford, John: Author of "Fredgehog." Publisher: Spindlewood (Barnstaple). Published in 1980.

Maggs, Colin Gordon: Author of "The Taunton and Barnstaple Line, Devon & Somerset Railway." Publisher: Oakwood Press (Trowbridge). Published in 1980.

Thompson, Vincent John: Author of "Everyone has telepathic abilities and healing powers." Publisher: V.J. Thompson (Barnstaple). Published in 1980.

1981

Barnstaple, A. G.: Author of "Hydrogen, a challenging opportunity: hydrogen supply: a report prepared for the Ontario Hydrogen Energy Task Force, volume 3." A.G. Barnstaple and A.J. Petrella, Ontario Hydro. Publisher: Ontario Hydrogen Task Force (Toronto). Published in 1981.

Kiddle, Catherine: Born in 1944, authored "What shall we do with the children?." Publisher: Spindlewood (Barnstaple). Published in 1981.

Linzell, Harold Harding: Born in 1895 and died in 1916, authored "Fallen on the Somme: the war diary of 2nd Lieutenant Harold Harding Linzell." Edited by M.A. Argyle. Publisher: M.A. Argyle (Barnstaple, North Devon). Published in 1981.

Orchard Theatre: Publication of "(Materials relating to Waiting for Godot, Orchard Theatre, Barnstaple, Devon touring production, 21 February - 22 May 1981)." Published in 1981.

1982

Barnstaple, A. G Petrella, A. J Ontario Hydro. Design and Development Division Ontario Hydro. Energy Studies and Development Dept: Publication of "Nuclear electrolytic hydrogen: a utility costing study." Energy Studies and Development Department; prepared by A.G. Barnstaple, A.J. Petrella; approved by R.E. Waters. Publisher: Design and Development Division (Toronto). Published in 1982.

Great Britain. Ordnance Survey: Publication of "Barnstaple and Ilfracombe (map): showing part of National Park." Publisher: Ordnance Survey (Southampton). Published in 1982.

Lowther, Kenneth Ernest: Born in 1931, authored "North Devon and Exmoor: Clovelly, Bideford, Barnstaple, Ilfracombe, Combe Martin, Lynton and Lynmouth, Minehead." Kenneth Lowther and Reginald Hammond. Publisher: Ward Lock (London). Published in 1982.

Ontario Hydrogen Energy Task Force: Publication of "Hydrogen supply: a report prepared for the Ontario Hydrogen Energy Task Force." A.G. Barnstaple and A.J. Petrella. --. Publisher: The Task Force (Toronto). Published in 1982.

Ordnance Survey: Publication of "Barnstaple and Ilfracombe: sheet no. 180." Publisher: Ordnance Survey (Southampton). Published in 1982.

Petrella, A. J Ontario Hydro. Design and Development Division Ontario Hydro. Energy Studies and Development Dept: Publication of "Hydrogen study. Volume 2, Electrolytic hydrogen in transportation." Energy Studies and Development Department; prepared by A.J. Petrella; reviewed by D. Chisholm, A.G. Barnstaple; approved by R.E. Waters Electrolytic hydrogen in transportation. Publisher: Design and Development Division (Toronto). Published in 1982.

Zimbabwe. National Archives: Publication of "(Material from the National Archives of Rhodesia on microfilm)." Publisher: Wessex Microfiling Ltd (Barnstaple, Devon). Published in 1982.

1983

Dodd, Lynley: Born in 1941, authored "Hairy Maclary from Donaldson's Dairy." Publisher: Spindlewood (Barnstaple). Published in 1983.

Lamplugh, Lois: Author of "Barnstaple, town on the Taw." Publisher: Phillimore (Chichester, Sussex). Published in 1983.

Leigh, Chris: Author of "Portrait of the Lynton & Barnstaple Railway." Publisher: Ian Allan (London). Published in 1983.

1984

Allfrey, Toni: Author of "Visitors guide to Barnstaple." Toni Allfrey, Tina Gaydon; photographs by Tina Gaydon. Publisher: fair Oak (Barnstaple). Published in 1984.

Estate Publications: Publisher of "Barnstaple (cartographic material): Ilfracombe, Bideford, Braunton. (Barnstaple Bideford Brauton Ifracombe)." Publisher: Estate Publishers (Tenterden, Kent). Published in 1984.

Graham, Amanda: Born in 1961, authored "Arthur." Written by Amanda Graham; illustrated by Donna Gynell. Publisher: Spindlewood

(Barnstaple). Published in 1984.

Petrella, A. J.: Author of "Remote community wind/diesel installation. Phase II, Fort Severn action plan." Prepared for the Ontario Ministry of Energy; prepared by A.J. Petrella; reviewed by D. Chisholm, A.G. Barnstaple. Publisher: Design and Development Division (Toronto). Published in 1984.

Shaida, Margaret: Author of "Views of Henley-on-Thames: a literary and pictorial selection." Publisher: Spindlewood (Barnstaple, Devon). Published in 1984.

Sutton, Eve: Author of "Surgeon's boy." Eve Sutton; illustrated by Fiona Kelly. Publisher: Spindlewood (Barnstaple, Devon). Published in 1984.

1985

Choe, In-hun: Author of "Gwang Jang." Translated into English, titled "The square" (translator: Kevin O'Rourke). Publisher: Spindlewood (Barnstaple). Published in 1985.

Choi, In-Hoon: Author of "The square." Choi In-Hoon; translated by Kevin O'Rourke. Publisher: Spindlewood (Barnstaple). Published in 1985.

Dodd, Lynley: Author of "The nickle nackle tree." Publisher: Spindlewood (Barnstaple (England)). Published in 1985.

Edmonds, E. A.: Born in 1927, authored "Geology of the country around Ilfracombe and Barnstaple memoir for 1:50,000 geological sheets 277 and 293, New Series." E.A. Edmonds, A. Whittaker and B.J. Williams; contributors J.M.C. Tombs ... (et al.). Publisher: H.M.S.O ((Swindon): National Environment Research Council; London). Published in 1985.

Heck, Elisabeth: Author of "Das andere Schaf." Translated into English, titled "The black sheep" (translator: Sita Jucker). Publisher: Spindlewood (Barnstaple). Published in 1985.

Jucker, Sita: Translator of "Das andere Schaf" by Elisabeth Heck into English ("The black sheep"). Publisher: Spindlewood (Barnstaple). Published in 1985.

O'Rourke, Kevin: Translator of "Gwang Jang" by In-hun Choe into English ("The square"). Publisher: Spindlewood (Barnstaple). Published in 1985.

Publication: Publication of "Horsepower." Publisher: Spindlewood (Barnstaple, (Devon)). Published in 1985.

Reed, Margaret A.: Author of "Pilton: its past and its people." Publisher: Vineyard Press (Barnstaple, Devon). Published in 1985.

Sutton, Eve: Author of "My cat likes to hide in boxes." By Eve Sutton; illustrated by Lynley Dodd. Publisher: Spindlewood (Barnstaple). Published in 1985.

Yuki, Shoji: Born in 1938, authored "I'm not a dog." Shoji Yuki; illustrated by Marie-Jose Sacre. Publisher: Spindlewood (Barnstaple). Published in 1985.

1986

Jackman, Leslie Arthur James: Author of "Freila finds a nest." Text by Leslie Jackman after an idea by Lieselotte Düngel-Gilles; illustrations by Dieter Müller. Publisher: Spindlewood (Barnstaple). Published in 1986.

Leeuwen, Wouter van: Author of "I can do it myself." Drawings, Wouter van Leeuwen; idea, Hans Elzenga. Publisher: Spindlewood (Barnstaple, Devon). Published in 1986.

1987

Common Wealth: Publisher of "Libertarian." Publisher: Common Wealth (Barnstaple). Published in 1987.

Fry, Andrew J.: Born in 1961, authored "Marionette." Andrew J. Fry; illustrations by K Morrish. Publisher: Andrew J. Fry (Barnstaple, N. Devon). Published in 1987.

1988

Bartlett, Tom: Author of "Postcard views of North Devon. Vol. 2, Barnstaple and around." Publisher: Badger Books (Bideford). Published in 1988.

Catchpole, L. T.: Author of "The Lynton and Barnstaple railway 1895-1935." Publisher: Oakwood Press (Oxford). Published in 1988.

Common Wealth: Publisher of "Common wealth: CW." Publisher: Common Wealth (Barnstaple, N. Devon). Published in 1988.

Maggs, Colin Gordon: Author of "The Barnstaple and Ilfracombe Railway." Publisher: Oakwood Press (Headington, Oxford). Published in 1988.

Northern Devon CVS: Publisher of "CALL: Caring Agencies Local List for Northern Devon." Devon Library Services; Northern Devon Council of Voluntary Services. Publisher: Northern Devon CVS (Barnstaple: Devon Library Services). Published in 1988.

1989

Alice: Publication of "Alice's diary: the memoirs of a cat." Publisher: chilton Designs (Barnstaple). Published in 1989.

Burrow: Publisher of "Barnstaple, Devon: town guide." Publisher: Burrow (London). Published in 1989.

David & Charles: Publisher of "The Lynton & Barnstaple Railway remembered." (compiled by) J.D.C.A. Prideaux. Publisher: David & Charles (Newton Abbot). Published in 1989.

North Devon Archaeological Society: Publisher of "North Devon watermills: based on a survey and record originally made in 1971-75 of some of the many mills and sites." By members of the North Devon Archaeological Society directed by Thomas E. Spencer. Revised, with historical and technical sections and a further list of mills added in 1989; edited by Josephine Thorpe. Publisher: North Devon Archaeological Society (Barnstaple). Published in 1989.

Patton, Jeffrey: Born in 1944, authored "Additives, adulterants and contaminants in beer." Publisher: Patton (Barnstaple). Published in 1989.

Prideaux, J. D. C. A.: Publication of "The Lynton & Barnstaple Railway remembered." J.D.C.A. Prideaux. Publisher: David & Charles (Newton Abbot, Devon). Published in 1989.

Terry, Richard: Born in 1964, authored "The Barnstaple clay tobacco pipe factory in the nineteenth century." Published in 1989.

1990

Alexander, Alan: Born in 1943, authored "Local government in the 1990s." Publisher: Philip Charles Media (Barnstaple). Published in 1990.

Ashdown, Paddy: Born in 1941, authored "The environment." Publisher: Philip Charles Media for Wroxton College (Barnstaple). Published in 1990.

Baldry, Tony: Born in 1950, authored "Social policy." Tony Baldry; Baroness Ewart-Biggs. Publisher: published for Wroxton College by Phillip Charles Media (Barnstaple). Published in 1990.

Baldwin, Nicholas: Author of "The Conservative Party: an instinct to survive." Publisher: Philip Charles Media for Wroxton College (Barnstaple). Published in 1990.

Budd, Stanley A.: Author of "Britain and the European Community: towards 1992 and beyond." Stanley Budd & Nicholas D.J. Baldwin. Publisher: Philip Charles Media for Wroxton College (Barnstaple). Published in 1990.

Concert Travel Company: Publisher of "Route." Publisher: Concert Travel Company (Barnstaple, Devon). Published in 1990.

Dodd, Lynley: Author of "The nickle nackle tree: a counting book." Publisher: Spindlewood (Barnstaple, Devon). Published in 1990.

Edgeler, Audrey: Author of "The art potters of Barnstaple." Publisher: Nimrod (Alton, Hants). Published in 1990.

Ezra, Derek, Baron: Publication of "Privatisation." Publisher: Philip Charles Media for Wroxton College (Barnstaple). Published in 1990.

Forman, Nigel: Author of "The National Health Service: "the debate"." Publisher: Phillip Charles Media (Barnstaple). Published in 1990.

George, Bruce: Author of "Defence and foreign affairs." Publisher: Philip Charles Media for Wroxton College (Barnstaple). Published in 1990.

Grantham, Cliff: Author of "Interest representation." Publisher: Philip Charles Media for Wroxton College (Barnstaple). Published in 1990.

Great Britain. National Rivers Authority. South West Region. Public Relations Section: Publication of "Barnstaple tidal defence scheme."

Publisher: NRA, South West Region, Public Relations Section (Exeter). Published in 1990.

Holmas, Stig: Author of "Son-of-thunder." By Stig Holmas; translated by Anne Born; illustrations by John Hurford. (Tordensønnen. English). Publisher: Spindlewood (Barnstaple). Published in 1990.

Holmås, Stig: Born in 1946, authored "Son-of-thunder." Stig Holmås; translated by Anne Born; illustrations by John Hurford. Publisher: Spindlewood (Barnstaple). Published in 1990.

Livingstone, Ken: Born in 1945, authored "Economic policy." Publisher: published for Wroxton College by Phillip Charles Media (Barnstaple). Published in 1990.

Mitchell, Austin Vernon: Born in 1934, authored "The Labour Party back from the brink." Publisher: Phillip Charles Media (Barnstaple). Published in 1990.

Nairne, Patrick, Sir: Publication of "The Civil Service: mandarins and ministers." Publisher: Philip Charles Media for Wroxton College (Barnstaple). Published in 1990.

Norton, Philip: Author of "The British constitution: a trans-Atlantic comparison." Publisher: Philip Charles Media for Wroxton College (Barnstaple). Published in 1990.

O'Leary, Brendan: Author of "The state of the union." Brendan O'Leary, Sir Anthony Meyer. Publisher: Philip Charles Media for Wroxton College (Barnstaple). Published in 1990.

Rush, Michael: Born in 1937, authored "The House of Commons." Publisher: Philip Charles Media for Wroxton College (Barnstaple). Published in 1990.

Westwood, Sallie: Author of "Gender and race: John Bull revisited." Publisher: Philip Charles Media for Wroxton College (Barnstaple). Published in 1990.

1991

Akers, Rosemary: Author of "The story of the Barnstaple Bridewell and Dornat's mineral water factory." By Rosemary Akers and Owen Friend. Publisher: The Authors (North Devon). Published in 1991.

Coleman, Vernon: Born in 1946, authored "How to overcome toxic stress and the twentieth century blues." Publisher: European Medical Journal (Barnstaple). Published in 1991.

Devon Library Services and the Northern Devon Council for Voluntary Service: Publisher of "Call 91: the Caring Agencies' local list." Compiled by the staff of the Reference Library, North Devon Library & Record Office, Barnstaple. Publisher: Devon Library Services and the Northern Devon Council for Voluntary Service (Exeter). Published in 1991.

Dodd, Lynley: Author of "Find me a tiger." Publisher: Spindlewood (Barnstaple, Devon). Published in 1991.

Masters, Jack: Author of "Passing the L.G.V. driving test: the new H.G.V regulations." Publisher: Patton (Barnstaple). Published in 1991.

Moore, Gerald: Born in 1926, authored "Fighting the developers." Gerald Moore and Adrian Moore. Publisher: Patton (Barnstaple). Published in 1991.

Spindlewood: Publisher of "Grandad's new old nursery rhymes." (compiled) by Merlin Jones; illustrated by Margaret Peters. Publisher: Spindlewood (Barnstaple, Devon). Published in 1991.

Warner, Bernard: Author of "North Devon: photographs to remember her by." Publisher: The Author (Barnstaple). Published in 1991.

1992

Coleman, Vernon: Born in 1946, authored "The Bilbury chronicles." Publisher: chilton Designs (Barnstaple). Published in 1992.

Mold, Ernest: Author of "Lynton and its coast: a brief history." Ernest Mold; illustrations by Edward Thornburgh. Publisher: Green Apple (Barnstaple). Published in 1992.

Nicholas, John: Author of "The North Devon line: the Exeter to Barnstaple railway from inception to the present day." Publisher: Oxford Pub. Co (Somerset). Published in 1992.

Publication: Publication of "Alice's adventures: the further memoirs of a cat." Publisher: chilton Designs (Barnstaple). Published in 1992.

1993

Coleman, Vernon: Born in 1946, authored "The man who inherited a golf course." Publisher: chilton Designs (Barnstaple). Published in 1993.

Coulter, James: Author of "The ancient chapels of North Devon." James Coulter; with photographs by the Author. Publisher: The Author (Barnstaple). Published in 1993.

Dunn, Sonja: Born in 1931, authored "Primary rhymerry: poems." By Sonja Dunn; illustrations by Mark Thurman. Publisher: Spindlewood (Markham, Ont. Pembroke Publishers; Barnstaple, Devon). Published in 1993.

Fry, Andrew J.: Born in 1961, authored "Breaking chains." Publisher: The Author (Barnstaple, N. Devon). Published in 1993.

Howells, Diane: Author of "The haunted glass." Publisher: Spindlewood (Barnstaple). Published in 1993.

Merrick, Anne: Author of "Someone came knocking." Publisher: Spindlewood (Barnstaple (England)). Published in 1993.

Mitchell, Victor: Born in 1937, authored "Exeter to Barnstaple Victor Mitchell and Keith Smith." Publisher: Middleton (Midhurst). Published in 1993.

Publication: Publication of "Barnstaple (cartographic material): Ilfracombe, Bideford, Braunton. (Barnstaple, Bideford, Braunton, Ilfracombe)." Publisher: Estate Publications, ca (Tenterden, Kent). Published in 1993.

1994

Burton, Roger A.: Author of "Simonsbath: the inside story of an Exmoor village." Publisher: Roger A. Burton (Barnstaple). Published in 1994.

Chugg, Brian: Author of "Aftermath of war: Brian Chugg: art works, 1944-54, The Museum of North Devon, The Square, Barnstaple, 20th August-30th September 1994." Publisher: North Devon District Council Museum of North Devon (Barnstaple). Published in 1994.

Coleman, Vernon: Born in 1946, authored "Bodypower: the secret of self-healing." Publisher: The European Medical Journal (Barnstaple, Devon). Published in 1994.

Dick, Uncle: Author of "Mr. Hooglegwank's petrol." By Uncle Dick; illustrated by Keira. Publisher: C & G (Barnstaple). Published in 1994.

Holmas, Stig: Born in 1946, authored "Apache Pass." Stig Holmas; translated by Anne Born; illustrations by John Hurford. Publisher: Spindlewood (Barnstaple). Published in 1994.

Keevill, Gwendoline: Author of "A selection of twelve Christian cameos." By Gwendoline Keevill; cover illustrations by Lorraine & Colin Bowman. Publisher: C & G Enterprises (Barnstaple). Published in 1994.

Manderley Press Limited: Publication of "Manderley street plan of Barnstaple (cartographic material)." Published in 1994.

North Devon Record Office: Publisher of "Sources for village history. 1, Bratton Fleming." Publisher: North Devon Record Office (Barnstaple). Published in 1994.

Ordnance Survey: Publication of "Barnstaple and Ilfracombe area: Sheet 180 2nd series." Publisher: Ordnance Survey (Southampton). Published in 1994.

Plantagenet Productions: Publisher of "Kinships: Gribbles of Barnstaple from church records, and the researches of Henry Edward Gribble and his cousins." Edited by his granddaughter (i.e. Dorothy Rose J. Gribble). Publisher: Plantagenet Productions (Newbury). Published in 1994.

Rowe, John: Author of "The North Devon yeomanry, 1794-1924." Publisher: North Devon District Council (Barnstaple). Published in 1994.

Squire, Terry: Author of "From slate to software: the story of a Devon village school." Publisher: T. & S.M. Squire (Barnstaple). Published in 1994.

St. Margaret's School; Barnstaple Newport School: Publisher of "Long, long, long, short, small, big poems." Compiled by Newport School and St. Margaret's School. Publisher: St. Margaret's School; Barnstaple Newport School (Torquay). Published in 1994.

1995

Adams, Chris: Born in 1945, authored "Land's End to Poole Bay." Publisher: Moor, Dale and

Mountain Press (Barnstaple). Published in 1995.

Barnstaple: It is a regular winner of the Britain in Bloom competition, in the category of 'Town', winning in 1995, 1997, 1999 and 2003. The town also won the Abbis Cup in 1996 and 1998 for Regional Supreme Champion (any size town), the Nations in Bloom - Best Town in the World in 1996, the Entente Florale - Best Town in Europe in 1996, and World in Bloom in 1998. [WP]

Burrows: Publisher of "Barnstaple: town guide." Publisher: Burrows (Wallington). Published in 1995.

Coleman, Vernon: Born in 1946, authored "Relief from IBS: simple steps for long-term control of irritable bowel syndrome." Publisher: European Medical Journal (Barnstaple). Published in 1995.

Ewart, Franzeska G.: Author of "Columbine." Publisher: Spindlewood (Barnstaple Devon). Published in 1995.

Harris, Herbert W.: Author of "Faith gymnasium: a story and study of faith." Publisher: Clinton (Barnstaple). Published in 1995.

Holmås, Stig: Author of "Fire wagons." Stig Holmås; translated by Anne Born; illustrations by John Hurford. Publisher: Spindlewood (Barnstaple). Published in 1995.

Kent, Timothy Arthur: Author of "Barnstaple silver and its makers." Publisher: J.H. Bourdon-Smith. Published in 1995.

McCrickard, Francis: Author of "The dead are listening." Publisher: Spindlewood (Barnstaple). Published in 1995.

Mitchell, Victor: Born in 1937, authored "Taunton to Barnstaple." Vic Mitchell and Keith Smith. Publisher: Middleton (Midhurst). Published in 1995.

North Devon District Council: Publication of "North Devon local plan: deposit plan November 1995." Publisher: North Devon District Council, Strategic Panning Unit (Barnstaple). Published in 1995.

Potter, Tessa: Author of "Dark waters." Publisher: Spindlewood (Barnstaple). Published in 1995.

1996

Charles E. Goad: Publisher of "(Goad shopping centre plan) (cartographic material): Barnstaple." Publisher: Charles E. Goad (Old Hatfield). Published in 1996.

Coleman, Vernon: Born in 1946, authored "Men in dresses: a study of transvestism/crossdressing." Publisher: European Medical Journal (Barnstaple). Published in 1996.

Devon Library Services: Publisher of "The Yeomanry." Publisher: Devon Library Services (Barnstaple). Published in 1996.

Dodd, Lynley: Author of "Hairy Maclary: six Lynley Dodd stories." Publisher: Spindlewood (Barnstaple (England)). Published in 1996.

Grant, Alison, Dr: Author of "Atlantic adventurer: John Delbridge of Barnstaple, 1564-1639." By Alison Grant; illustrations editor, Peter Ferguson. Publisher: A. Grant (Instow). Published in 1996.

Holma°s, Stig: Author of "The people of the rising sun." Stig Ho°lmas; translated by Anne Born; illustrations by John Hulford. (Soloppgangens folk. English). Publisher: Spindlewood (Barnstaple). Published in 1996.

Merrick, Anne: Author of "Hannah's ghost." Publisher: Spindlewood (Barnstaple, (England)). Published in 1996.

North Devon District Council, Strategic Planning Unit: Publisher of "North Devon local plan: environmental appraisal of the deposit plan." Publisher: North Devon District Council, Strategic Planning Unit (Barnstaple). Published in 1996.

North Devon Museums Service: Publisher of "North Devon at war." Publisher: North Devon Museums Service (Barnstaple: Devon Library Services). Published in 1996.

Norton Publishing Ltd: Publisher of "Classic walks: Devon: 60 circular routes, includes Dartmoor." Publisher: Norton Publishing Ltd (Barnstaple). Published in 1996.

Rowe, John: Author of "The Sixth Devons and their origins." Publisher: North Devon District Council (Barnstaple). Published in 1996.

1997

Allen, Judith: Born in 1984, authored "Historical paper dolls: mediaeval." Text and artwork, Judith Allen. Publisher: Elisheva (Barnstaple). Published in 1997.

Coleman, Vernon: Born in 1946, authored "Dr Vernon Coleman's fast action health secrets 1001 invaluable health tips and home remedies." Publisher: European Medical Journal (Barnstaple). Published in 1997.

Estate Publications: Publisher of "Barnstaple (cartographic material): Bideford, Braunton, Ilfracombe, Northam." Publisher: Estate Publishers (Kent). Published in 1997.

Karczmarz, Eva: Born in 1930, authored "Wisienka: a little Polish girl tells her own true story!1939-1942." Publisher: C & G Enterprises (Barnstaple). Published in 1997.

1998

Coleman, Vernon: Born in 1946, authored "The story of medicine." Publisher: European Medical Journal (Barnstaple). Published in 1998.

Devonshire Association: Publisher of "The lost chronicle of Barnstaple 1586-1611." Edited with an introduction by Todd Gray. Publisher: Devonshire Association (Exeter). Published in 1998.

Estate: Publisher of "Barnstaple, Bideford, Braunton, Ilfracombe, Northam." Publisher: Estate (Tenterden). Published in 1998.

Flemington, Richard: Author of "Monte Cassino: they came to a monastery." Publisher: Prospectus House (Barnstaple). Published in 1998.

Gray, Todd: Author of "The lost chronicle of Barnstaple 1586 - 1611." Publisher: The Devonshire Association (Exeter). Published in 1998.

Loveday, Pete: Author of "Big trip travel agency. 3: looking forward looking back." Publisher: P. Loveday (Barnstaple). Published in 1998.

1999

Coleman, Vernon: Born in 1946, authored "Animal rights, human wrongs: a blueprint for a better society." Publisher: Blue Books (Barnstaple). Published in 1999.

2000

Coleman, Vernon: Born in 1946, authored "The 101 sexiest, craziest, most outrageous agony column questions (and answers) of all time." Vernon Coleman; edited by Donna Antoinette Davidson. Publisher: Blue Books (Barnstaple). Published in 2000.

Cornwall & Devon Media: Publisher of "Cornwall from the air 2000." Publisher: Cornwall & Devon Media (Barnstaple). Published in 2000.

Estate Publications: Publisher of "Barnstaple, Ilfracombe, Bideford, Braunton, Northam (cartographic material): Street maps with index & postcodes." Publisher: Estate Publishers (Tenterden). Published in 2000.

Sims, Patricia: Author of "Personality checklist." Publisher: Mortimore Books (Barnstaple). Published in 2000.

2001

Broad, Joan Earle: Born in 1945, authored "Charlie's surprise." By Joan Earle Broad; illustrated by Pauline V. Caddie. Publisher: J.E. Broad (Barnstaple). Published in 2001.

Coleman, Vernon: Author of "How to make money while watching TV: how you can become financially independent through publishing in three easy steps and less than six months: everything you need to know about how to turn ideas into books and books into money." Publisher: Blue Books (Barnstaple). Published in 2001.

Groen, Els de: Author of "No roof in Bosnia." Els de Groen; translated by Patricia Crampton. Publisher: Spindlewood (Barnstaple). Published in 2001.

Needham, Dennis: Author of "Francis Frith's around Barnstaple." Publisher: Frith Book Co (Salisbury). Published in 2001.

2002

A361 road: The section from Barnstaple to the M5 near Tiverton has been designated the North Devon Link Road, and enables relatively fast access to north Devon and Bude, Cornwall, relieving pressure on the A39 and A358. This section is a modern, wide single-carriageway trunk road (which was de-trunked in 2002), apart from the 5-mile stretch between Tiverton and the M5, which is dual-carriageway. The rest of the road, from Taunton to Rugby, is largely county-road class; the quality of the road surface, width and verges can sometimes be barely better than a B-road. [WP]

Beal, George H.: Born in 1911, authored "The chequered life of George Beal: a Devonian." Publisher: G. Beal (Barnstaple). Published in 2002.

Beazley, Marga H. C.: Author of "Poems about life and living." Publisher: M.H.C. Beazley (Barnstaple). Published in 2002.

Coleman, Vernon: Author of "Paris in my springtime." Publisher: chilton Designs (Barnstaple). Published in 2002.

2003

Adams, Chris: Born in 1945, authored "Circular walks from Ringstead Bay." Publisher: Christopher Adams (Barnstaple). Published in 2003.

Coleman, Vernon: Born in 1946, authored "England our England: a nation in jeopardy sound reasons to reject the euro and the EU." Publisher: Blue Books (Barnstaple). Published in 2003.

Publication: Publication of "Full colour street map of Barnstaple, Bideford, Braunton, Lynton, Great Torrington, Holsworthy, Ilfracombe, South Molton, Combe Martin, Woolacombe." Published in 2003.

Stone, Avril: Author of "Book of Barnstaple. Vol. 2, from coronation to millennium." Published in 2003.

2004

Coleman, Vernon: Author of "Confronting the global bully: why America is Britain's real enemy, why the 'Special Relationship' is dangerous and action you must take." Publisher: Blue Books (Barnstaple). Published in 2004.

Goldeneye Map-Guides: Publication of "Exmoor, North Devon, The Quantocks: mountain bike routes." Edited, designed and published by Goldeneye. Publisher: Goldeneye (Barnstaple). Published in 2004.

Teague, Denise: Author of "Barnstaple: a history and celebration of the town." Denise Teague and Elizabeth Hammett. Publisher: Frith (Salisbury). Published in 2004.

2005

Catchpole, L. T.: Author of "The Lynton & Barnstaple railway 1895-1935." By L.T. Catchpole. (Lynton and Barnstaple railway 1895-1935). Publisher: Oakwood (Usk). Published in 2005.

Goldeneye Map-Guides: Publication of "Dartmoor, south Devon: cycling country lanes & byways." Edited, designed and published by Goldeneye. Publisher: Goldeneye (Barnstaple). Published in 2005.

Ordnance Survey: Publication of "Bideford, Ilfracombe & Barnstaple (cartographic material)." Publisher: Ordnance Survey (Southampton). Published in 2005.

2006

Coleman, Vernon: Author of "Living in a Fascist country: conspiracies, peak oil, greedy politicians, endless religious wars and your disappearing freedom and privacy." Publisher: Blue Books (Barnstaple). Published in 2006.

Geographers' A-Z Map Company: Publisher of "A-Z Barnstaple." Publisher: Geographers' A-Z Map Company (Sevenoaks). Published in 2006.

Goldeneye Map-Guides: Publication of "Cycling country lanes & byways: Pembrokeshire, West Wales = Sir Benfro A Gorllewin Cymru." Edited, designed and published by Goldeneye. Publisher: Goldeneye (Barnstaple). Published in 2006.

2008

Parker, Philip M.: INSEAD Chair Professor of Management Science. On September 4, 2007 he obtained the patent for a "Method and Apparatus for Automated Authoring and Marketing," which was used, in 2008, to create "Barnstaple: Webster's Timeline History." Publisher: ICON Group International, Inc. (San Diego). Abstract: The present invention provides for the automatic authoring, marketing, and/or distributing of title material. A computer automatically authors material. The material is automatically formatted into a desired format, resulting in a title material. The title material may also be automatically distributed to a recipient. Meta material, marketing material, and control material are automatically authored and if desired, distributed to a recipient. Further, the title material may be authored on demand, such that it may be in any desired language and with the latest version and content.

License for Wikipedia Entries

The GNU Free Documentation License does not apply to entries in the public domain, used under commercial license, or under copyright. For each entry or "Document" (as defined below) used from www.wikipedia.org the GNU Free Documentation License applies, the text of which is provided here. To retrieve the original Wikipedia article via the internet, use the url www.en.wikipedia.org/wiki/HEADWORD where "HEADWORD" is the headword provided before the entry. For example, a Wikipedia article for "Apple Pie" is http://en.wikipedia.org/wiki/Apple_Pie. Note that expression words are separated by underscores (e.g. Apple_Pie). Electronic backup copies of these articles are available from www.websters-online-dictionary.org; type the headword into the search box to locate the backup. Paperback versions of this book are being printed on demand, in unknown quantities. ICON Group International, Inc. makes no warrantees with respect to any of the content in this book.

Text of the GNU Free Documentation License

Version 1.2, November 2002; Copyright (C) 2000,2001,2002 Free Software Foundation, Inc. 51 Franklin St, Fifth Floor, Boston, MA 02110-1301 USA. Everyone is permitted to copy and distribute verbatim copies of this license document, but changing it is not allowed.

0. PREAMBLE

The purpose of this License is to make a manual, textbook, or other functional and useful document "free" in the sense of freedom: to assure everyone the effective freedom to copy and redistribute it, with or without modifying it, either commercially or noncommercially. Secondarily, this License preserves for the author and publisher a way to get credit for their work, while not being considered responsible for modifications made by others. This License is a kind of "copyleft", which means that derivative works of the document must themselves be free in the same sense. It complements the GNU General Public License, which is a copyleft license designed for free software. We have designed this License in order to use it for manuals for free software, because free software needs free documentation: a free program should come with manuals providing the same freedoms that the software does. But this License is not limited to software manuals; it can be used for any textual work, regardless of subject matter or whether it is published as a printed book. We recommend this License principally for works whose purpose is instruction or reference.

1. APPLICABILITY AND DEFINITIONS

This License applies to any manual or other work, in any medium, that contains a notice placed by the copyright holder saying it can be distributed under the terms of this License. Such a notice grants a world-wide, royalty-free license, unlimited in duration, to use that work under the conditions stated herein. The "Document", below, refers to any such manual or work. Any member of the public is a licensee, and is addressed as "you". You accept the license if you copy, modify or distribute the work in a way requiring permission under copyright law. A "Modified Version" of the Document means any work containing the Document or a portion of it, either copied verbatim, or with modifications and/or translated into another language. A "Secondary Section" is a named appendix or a front-matter section of the Document that deals exclusively with the relationship of the publishers or authors of the Document to the Document's overall subject (or to related matters) and contains nothing that could fall directly within that overall subject. (Thus, if the Document is in part a textbook of mathematics, a Secondary Section may not explain any mathematics.) The relationship could be a matter of historical connection with the subject or with related matters, or of legal, commercial, philosophical, ethical or political position regarding them. The "Invariant Sections" are certain Secondary Sections whose titles are designated, as being those of Invariant Sections, in the notice that says that the Document is released under this License. If a section does not fit the above definition of Secondary then it is not allowed to be designated as Invariant. The Document may contain zero Invariant Sections. If the Document does not identify any Invariant Sections then there are none. The "Cover Texts" are certain short passages of text that are listed, as Front-Cover Texts or Back-Cover Texts, in the notice that says that the Document is released under this License. A Front-Cover Text may be at most 5 words, and a Back-Cover Text may be at most 25 words. A "Transparent" copy of the Document means a machine-readable copy, represented in a format whose specification is available to the general public, that is suitable for revising the document straightforwardly with generic text editors or (for images composed of pixels) generic paint programs or (for drawings) some widely available drawing editor, and that is suitable for input to text formatters or for automatic translation to a variety of formats suitable for input to text formatters. A copy made in an otherwise Transparent file format whose markup, or absence of markup, has been arranged to thwart or discourage subsequent modification by readers is not Transparent. An image format is not Transparent if used for any substantial amount of text. A copy that is not "Transparent" is called "Opaque". Examples of suitable formats for Transparent copies include plain ASCII without markup, Texinfo input format, LaTeX input format, SGML or XML using a publicly available DTD, and standard-conforming simple HTML, PostScript or PDF designed for human modification. Examples of transparent image formats include PNG, XCF and JPG. Opaque formats include proprietary formats that can be read and edited only by proprietary word processors, SGML or XML for which the DTD and/or processing tools are not generally available, and the machine-generated HTML, PostScript or PDF produced by some word processors for output purposes only. The "Title Page" means, for a printed book, the title page itself, plus such following pages as are needed to hold, legibly, the material this License requires to appear in the title page. For works in formats which do not have any title page as such, "Title Page" means the text near the most prominent appearance of the work's title, preceding the beginning of the body of the text. A section "Entitled XYZ" means a named subunit of the Document whose title either is precisely XYZ or contains XYZ in parentheses following text that translates XYZ in another language. (Here XYZ stands for a specific section name mentioned below, such as "Acknowledgements", "Dedications", "Endorsements", or "History".) To "Preserve the Title" of such a section when you modify the Document means that it remains a section "Entitled XYZ" according to this definition. The Document may include Warranty Disclaimers next to the notice which states that this License applies to the Document. These Warranty Disclaimers are considered to be included by reference in this License, but only as regards disclaiming warranties: any other implication that these Warranty Disclaimers may have is void and has no effect on the meaning of this License.

2. VERBATIM COPYING

You may copy and distribute the Document in any medium, either commercially or noncommercially, provided that this License, the copyright notices, and the license notice saying this License applies to the Document are reproduced in all copies, and that you add no other conditions whatsoever to those of this License. You may not use technical measures to obstruct or control the reading or further copying of the copies you make or distribute. However, you may accept compensation in exchange for copies. If you distribute a large enough number of copies you must also follow the conditions in section 3. You may also lend copies, under the same conditions stated above, and you may publicly display copies.

3. COPYING IN QUANTITY

If you publish printed copies (or copies in media that commonly have printed covers) of the Document, numbering more than 100, and the Document's license notice requires Cover Texts, you must enclose the copies in covers that carry, clearly and legibly, all these Cover Texts: Front-Cover Texts on the front cover, and Back-Cover Texts on the back cover. Both covers must also clearly and legibly identify you as the publisher of these copies. The front cover must present the full title with all words of the title equally prominent and visible. You may add other material on the covers in addition. Copying with changes limited to the covers, as long as they preserve the title of the Document and satisfy these conditions, can be treated as verbatim copying in other respects. If the required texts for either cover are too voluminous to fit legibly, you should put the first ones listed (as many as fit reasonably) on the actual cover, and continue the rest onto adjacent pages. If you publish or distribute Opaque copies of the Document numbering more than 100, you must either include a machine-readable Transparent copy along with each Opaque copy, or state in or with each Opaque copy a computer-network location from which the general network-using public has access to download using public-standard network protocols a complete Transparent copy of the Document, free of added material. If you use the latter option, you must take reasonably prudent steps, when you begin distribution of Opaque copies in quantity, to ensure that this Transparent copy will remain thus accessible at the stated location until at least one year after the last time you distribute an Opaque copy (directly or through your agents or retailers) of that edition to the public. It is requested, but not required, that you contact the authors of the Document well before redistributing any large number of copies, to give them a chance to provide you with an updated version of the Document.

4. MODIFICATIONS

You may copy and distribute a Modified Version of the Document under the conditions of sections 2 and 3 above, provided that you release the Modified Version under precisely this License, with the Modified Version filling the role of the Document, thus licensing distribution and modification of the Modified Version to whoever possesses a copy of it. In addition, you must do these things in the Modified Version:

A. Use in the Title Page (and on the covers, if any) a title distinct from that of the Document, and from those of previous versions (which should, if there were any, be listed in the History section of the Document). You may use the same title as a previous version if the original publisher of that version gives permission.

B. List on the Title Page, as authors, one or more persons or entities responsible for authorship of the modifications in the Modified Version, together with at least five of the principal authors of the Document (all of its principal authors, if it has fewer than five), unless they release you from this requirement.

C. State on the Title page the name of the publisher of the Modified Version, as the publisher.
D. Preserve all the copyright notices of the Document.
E. Add an appropriate copyright notice for your modifications adjacent to the other copyright notices.
F. Include, immediately after the copyright notices, a license notice giving the public permission to use the Modified Version under the terms of this License, in the form shown in the Addendum below.
G. Preserve in that license notice the full lists of Invariant Sections and required Cover Texts given in the Document's license notice.
H. Include an unaltered copy of this License.
I. Preserve the section Entitled "History", Preserve its Title, and add to it an item stating at least the title, year, new authors, and publisher of the Modified Version as given on the Title Page. If there is no section Entitled "History" in the Document, create one stating the title, year, authors, and publisher of the Document as given on its Title Page, then add an item describing the Modified Version as stated in the previous sentence.
J. Preserve the network location, if any, given in the Document for public access to a Transparent copy of the Document, and likewise the network locations given in the Document for previous versions it was based on. These may be placed in the "History" section. You may omit a network location for a work that was published at least four years before the Document itself, or if the original publisher of the version it refers to gives permission.
K. For any section Entitled "Acknowledgements" or "Dedications", Preserve the Title of the section, and preserve in the section all the substance and tone of each of the contributor acknowledgements and/or dedications given therein.
L. Preserve all the Invariant Sections of the Document, unaltered in their text and in their titles. Section numbers or the equivalent are not considered part of the section titles.
M. Delete any section Entitled "Endorsements". Such a section may not be included in the Modified Version.
N. Do not retitle any existing section to be Entitled "Endorsements" or to conflict in title with any Invariant Section.
O. Preserve any Warranty Disclaimers.

If the Modified Version includes new front-matter sections or appendices that qualify as Secondary Sections and contain no material copied from the Document, you may at your option designate some or all of these sections as invariant. To do this, add their titles to the list of Invariant Sections in the Modified Version's license notice. These titles must be distinct from any other section titles. You may add a section Entitled "Endorsements", provided it contains nothing but endorsements of your Modified Version by various parties--for example, statements of peer review or that the text has been approved by an organization as the authoritative definition of a standard. You may add a passage of up to five words as a Front-Cover Text, and a passage of up to 25 words as a Back-Cover Text, to the end of the list of Cover Texts in the Modified Version. Only one passage of Front-Cover Text and one of Back-Cover Text may be added by (or through arrangements made by) any one entity. If the Document already includes a cover text for the same cover, previously added by you or by arrangement made by the same entity you are acting on behalf of, you may not add another; but you may replace the old one, on explicit permission from the previous publisher that added the old one. The author(s) and publisher(s) of the Document do not by this License give permission to use their names for publicity for or to assert or imply endorsement of any Modified Version.

5. COMBINING DOCUMENTS

You may combine the Document with other documents released under this License, under the terms defined in section 4 above for modified versions, provided that you include in the combination all of the Invariant Sections of all of the original documents, unmodified, and list them all as Invariant Sections of your combined work in its license notice, and that you preserve all their Warranty Disclaimers. The combined work need only contain one copy of this License, and multiple identical Invariant Sections may be replaced with a single copy. If there are multiple Invariant Sections with the same name but different contents, make the title of each such section unique by adding at the end of it, in parentheses, the name of the original author or publisher of that section if known, or else a unique number. Make the same adjustment to the section titles in the list of Invariant Sections in the license notice of the combined work. In the combination, you must combine any sections Entitled "History" in the various original documents, forming one section Entitled "History"; likewise combine any sections Entitled "Acknowledgements", and any sections Entitled "Dedications". You must delete all sections Entitled "Endorsements."

6. COLLECTIONS OF DOCUMENTS

You may make a collection consisting of the Document and other documents released under this License, and replace the individual copies of this License in the various documents with a single copy that is included in the collection, provided that you follow the rules of this License for verbatim copying of each of the documents in all other respects. You may extract a single document from such a collection, and distribute it individually under this License, provided you insert a copy of this License into the extracted document, and follow this License in all other respects regarding verbatim copying of that document.

7. AGGREGATION WITH INDEPENDENT WORKS

A compilation of the Document or its derivatives with other separate and independent documents or works, in or on a volume of a storage or distribution medium, is called an "aggregate" if the copyright resulting from the compilation is not used to limit the legal rights of the compilation's users beyond what the individual works permit. When the Document is included in an aggregate, this License does not apply to the other works in the aggregate which are not themselves derivative works of the Document. If the Cover Text requirement of section 3 is applicable to these copies of the Document, then if the Document is less than one half of the entire aggregate, the Document's Cover Texts may be placed on covers that bracket the Document within the aggregate, or the electronic equivalent of covers if the Document is in electronic form. Otherwise they must appear on printed covers that bracket the whole aggregate.

8. TRANSLATION

Translation is considered a kind of modification, so you may distribute translations of the Document under the terms of section 4. Replacing Invariant Sections with translations requires special permission from their copyright holders, but you may include translations of some or all Invariant Sections in addition to the original versions of these Invariant Sections. You may include a translation of this License, and all the license notices in the Document, and any Warranty Disclaimers, provided that you also include the original English version of this License and the original versions of those notices and disclaimers. In case of a disagreement between the translation and the original version of this License or a notice or disclaimer, the original version will prevail. If a section in the Document is Entitled "Acknowledgements", "Dedications", or "History", the requirement (section 4) to Preserve its Title (section 1) will typically require changing the actual title.

9. TERMINATION

You may not copy, modify, sublicense, or distribute the Document except as expressly provided for under this License. Any other attempt to copy, modify, sublicense or distribute the Document is void, and will automatically terminate your rights under this License. However, parties who have received copies, or rights, from you under this License will not have their licenses terminated so long as such parties remain in full compliance.

10. FUTURE REVISIONS OF THIS LICENSE

The Free Software Foundation may publish new, revised versions of the GNU Free Documentation License from time to time. Such new versions will be similar in spirit to the present version, but may differ in detail to address new problems or concerns. See http://www.gnu.org/copyleft/. Each version of the License is given a distinguishing version number. If the Document specifies that a particular numbered version of this License "or any later version" applies to it, you have the option of following the terms and conditions either of that specified version or of any later version that has been published (not as a draft) by the Free Software Foundation. If the Document does not specify a version number of this License, you may choose any version ever published (not as a draft) by the Free Software Foundation.

How to use this License for your documents

To use this License in a document you have written, include a copy of the License in the document and put the following copyright and license notices just after the title page: Copyright (c) YEAR YOUR NAME. Permission is granted to copy, distribute and/or modify this document under the terms of the GNU Free Documentation License, Version 1.2 or any later version published by the Free Software Foundation; with no Invariant Sections, no Front-Cover Texts, and no Back-Cover Texts. A copy of the license is included in the section entitled "GNU Free Documentation License". If you have Invariant Sections, Front-Cover Texts and Back-Cover Texts, replace the "with...Texts." line with this: with the Invariant Sections being LIST THEIR TITLES, with the Front-Cover Texts being LIST, and with the Back-Cover Texts being LIST. If you have Invariant Sections without Cover Texts, or some other combination of the three, merge those two alternatives to suit the situation. If your document contains nontrivial examples of program code, we recommend releasing these examples in parallel under your choice of free software license, such as the GNU General Public License, to permit their use in free software.

Index

D

E

F

G

1504080R0

Printed in Great Britain by
Amazon.co.uk, Ltd.,
Marston Gate.